T0159626

BEETHOVEN IN DENVER

AND OTHER POEMS

Also by Burton Raffel

Poetry

Man as a Social Animal 1986
Evenly Distributed Rubble 1985
Grice 1985
Changing the Angle of the Sun-Dial 1984
Four Humours 1979
Mia Poems 1968

Fiction

Founder's Fortune (with Elizabeth Raffel) 1989
Founder's Fury (with Elizabeth Raffel) 1988
After Such Ignorance 1986
Short Story 3 (with Robert Creeley, et al.) 1960

Criticism

The Annotated Milton 1999
The Art of Translating Prose 1994
From Stress to Stress: An Autobiography of English Prosody 1992
Artists All: Creativity, the University and the World 1991
The Art of Translating Poetry 1988
Politicians, Poets and Con Men 1986
Ezra Pound: The Prime Minister of Poetry 1985
American Victorians: Explorations in Emotional History 1984
How to Read a Poem 1984
T. S. Eliot 1982
Robert Lowell 1981
Why Re-Create? 1973
The Forked Tongue: A Study of the Translation Process 1971
Introduction to Poetry 1971
The Development of Modern Indonesian Poetry 1967

Anthologies

The Signet Classic Book of Contemporary American Stories 1986
The Signet Classic Book of American Stories 1985
Possum and Ole Ez In the Public Eye 1985
Forty-One Stories of O. Henry 1984
Poems 1971

BEETHOVEN IN DENVER

A N D   O T H E R   P O E M S

BY

BURTON RAFFEL

CONUNDRUM

PRESS

Published in 1999 in the United States of America by Conundrum
Press, Crested Butte, Colorado.

Cover photograph by Glen R. Swearingen ©.

ISBN 0-9657159-6-5 (cloth) – ISBN 0-9657159-4-9 (pbk.)

Library of Congress Catalog Number 99-75271

For Aryeh Mordechai Pride

CONTENTS

BEETHOVEN IN DENVER

OTHER POEMS

BEETHOVEN IN DENVER

How It All Started

Would Beethoven be happy, offered a candy bar?
Would he chew on sticky peanuts
And hymn out a chocolatey choral prelude,
Or take just one bite and deliver himself of a
      sharp-tongued fugue?
(I'm talking about Beethoven—the musician—yes, him.
I mean Ludwig Van Beethoven, Luigi da Beethoven,
Louis de Beethoven—because of course he signed his
      name in all those ways.)
And then I decided that after a hundred and fifty years,
And in a world which sometimes seems to us even
      more insane than the one he knew
And which he too thought mad,
Beethoven would risk anything
And so would I.
"Liebe Herr Beethoven, your candy bar."
"Danke schön, Herr Raffel."

TIME

We were sitting out in the backyard, in three lawn chairs,
The barbecue shining hot in the already hot sun,
A piña colada in everyone's hand—my wife makes
       great piña coladas,
Famous all over Denver—and I asked him
Why had he taken so long to get to the *Ninth Symphony*.
He bellowed, slapped his lag, nearly spilled his drink:
"Ach, you Americans! So long, eh! Listen, I wasn't
       quite sixty when I died.
How much time did I have? It all came easy to
       that Mozart,
Even to old Papa Haydn—I know, I was there!—but
       nothing came easy to me."
He sipped his drink and smiled at my wife:
Clearly, he had not lost his taste for alcohol
Or for pretty women.
"You have to know how to work,
You have to be patient,
You have to wait."
The steaks were done—everyone wanted them rare—
And I got up to serve, two of my dogs, the little ones,
       trotting after me.
But the third one, the big part-Labrador, Midnight we
       named her,
Lay quietly under his chair, and his square left hand
       moved back and forth,
Stroking her fur. He liked that, I could see he liked
       that a lot—
He was said to be a tactile, sensuous guy even then—

So I took my time with the steaks and let him enjoy
        the dog, and the drink, and my wife's lovely smile.
A hundred and fifty years is a long time to wait
Even for a patient man
To whom nothing came easy.

Mountains

"I like your Rocky Mountains—such a name!
They are not so big as the Alps,
But I like them."
It takes a certain nerve to contradict Beethoven,
Even about mountains.
"They're *bigger* than the Alps,
Herr Beethoven. You see, it all depends on where
       you're standing."
He leaned on my cedar fence, grinning.
"It does, doesn't it? Very good, Herr Raffel,
I will remember that pregnant, that very pregnant
       observation.
Very good!"
I wasn't sure that I really ought to smile, but anyway
       I did.
"Thank you, Herr Beethoven."
But he was staring off at the Rockies and I know he
       did not hear me
And I was not about to interrupt.

MOTHERS

My mother called, long distance.
I could not tell her Beethoven was in the house:
She was European-born herself, there was no nonsense
        in her
In such matters. "I'm fine, I'm fine," I assured her.
"The children are fine.
Elizabeth is fine.
The dogs are fine."
She was fine too.
All the same, when I hung up I was sweating.

FREEDOM

"But where are your passports?" he asked, after I'd
     built him a fire in our tiny fireplace,
Even though it was far too warm for a fire. He missed
     fires, he said,
And how could I not be obliging? "I have been here
     some days and never seen your passports."
"Upstairs, in my desk somewhere," I smiled. "We use
     them only for travel abroad."
He shook his head: "No one asks to see them?
The Polizei don't stop you on the street?"
I hesitated only a moment. "Only if we're jay-walking,"
I answered, and immediately thought better of it—
     too late, of course.
I was always putting my foot in my mouth, with him.
But he was not bothered. "How free you are!" he
     exclaimed softly,
Turning and staring into the fire, his drink forgotten in
     his hand.
"How wonderful to be so free! How I envy you!"
He spoke with a kind of hushed deliberateness
And behind the words I could hear the music, inchoate
     still but already starting to swell up once again.
What will he do? I asked myself, with something a
     little like fear.
What will he do, now that he's back?

SCIENCE AND ECOLOGY

There were many things I suspected he would never
      understand
And so to keep the peace I never mentioned them
Unless he'd found out independently and then come
      to me
For enlightenment—or, at least, for information.
Men on the moon, for example, and space ships
      and shuttles,
And nuclear bombs, and the slaughter of Tasmanians
And baby seals: a man from another time
Could not be expected to adjust to our changed ways
In much a of a hurry. Al Capone? Richard Nixon?
Continental drift? I knew I could never explain,
And worked hard at saying not a god damned thing
      about any of them.

NAPOLEON

"It's not that I *disliked* the man—
He did not think of himself as a man:
He fooled me, for years—fooled many of us; indeed,
        some never caught on—
With all that French Revolution talk: liberté, egalité,
        fraternité.
Those were words that pierced our hearts,
And he used them just as well as he used his soldiers,
Maybe better. We believed him—all across Europe
        we believed him,
Trusted him, fought for him.
Millions died: did you know that?
Who before your twentieth century killed as many
        human beings as Napoleon did?
        Genghis Khan, perhaps?
        But who else?
No, he did not really see himself as human, but
        superhuman—
Years before Nietszche saw anything.
We were only instruments, little toy machines to
        play him the tunes he heard in his mind.
It would have been an incredible orchestra, you know,
        but he got everything confused with those
        Russian harmonies,
And the dissonance brought him down, kept him
        down—yes, despite the Hundred Days,
And all that. But consonance could not have
        helped him.
He might have studied orchestration sooner,
        perhaps he could have perfected his notation;

10

He was always a first-rate conductor.
No, the dissonances were not what destroyed him;
Please, make that clear when you write this down.
It was his French syncopation, that heartless,
       egotistical little waltz.
He expected all the world to dance it, wound tight
       in his elegant arms.
But France is not a musical country, thank God,
And even his own people would not tuck up their
       skirts for him, not for what he offered them."

SHOW-AND-TELL

My younger daughter, a fifth grader,
Is of course too advanced for elementary
      show-and-tell,
But not too advanced for pride: our house guest
      became her favorite recess and lunchroom
      conversation,
And the other little girls became curious, and even
      their teacher got involved and very
      curious indeed.
"Shifra," Miss Clark suggested one day, "why don't you
      invite Mr. Beethoven to come to our class?
Everyone here would like to meet him: we've heard
      so much about him
From you." "Sure," Shifra agreed, happy to have
      the chance,
And she came home that afternoon and approached
      Beethoven almost before she took her coat off
And inevitably Beethoven said yes: he never turned
      down an opportunity.
"It wasn't very good, for a while," Shifra reported
      that night.
"I mean he talked about freedom, and Napoleon—who's
      Napoleon, Daddy?—
And then he played us some of his music, but the
      piano was out of tune
And he was out of practice
And the music didn't sound cool.
And we all got restless—you know how little
      kids are—

And Miss Clark, you could just see she didn't know
      what to say to someone like him,
And I was wishing, really I was, that I hadn't ever
      mentioned his name.
Really, Daddy: you have to understand that grown-ups
      can be very boring,
Even great ones like Mr. Beethoven.
But luckily Heather Harris had her violin with her,
      she had a lesson that afternoon,
And when Beethoven saw it, suddenly, he asked her
      if he could play it a little
And she said sure, he could, if he was careful—
And he really could play it, too, he played all kinds
      of dance tunes,
And if we hummed him a song he played that too,
And we all started to dance, and Miss Clark danced
      too, she was very happy,
And even the principal came in and he ended up
      dancing with us,
And almost the whole school danced, we went up and
      down the halls in a great big line
And we went out on the lawn
And that was why it turned out okay, in the end, it
      really did.
He was kind of like the Pied Piper, Daddy, if you
      know what I mean."
I told her I knew exactly what she meant, tucked her
      in, kissed her,
And she was asleep almost before I left the room;
      she'd danced a great deal, she was all tired out.
But by the time she was closing her eyes Beethoven
      and I were sitting in the living room,

Discussing nineteenth-century Austrian politics
And the Emperor Francis' sexual indiscretions.
Before we too went to bed we had gotten around to
      poor Franz Schubert
And I had told him many stories about Richard
      Wagner: he could tell right away,
Even talking to a non-musician like me, that Wagner
      was the key to what had happened after his
      own death,
And he was fascinated, insatiable. "Tomorrow," I
      promised, getting too tired to go on,
"Tomorrow I'll play you *Tristan und Isolde*. The whole
      thing. I promise."
"On the piano?" he wondered—and I saw at once that
      we had even more to discuss
Than I had realized. "You'll see," I put him off—it was
      too much to tackle at that hour,
Tired as I was. "Or maybe I ought to say, you'll *hear*."
He laughed, I'd always known he'd have a superb
      sense of humor.
"Very well," he agreed. "Aufwiederhören." And I
      laughed too,
Though he did not know why.

EASTERN LIGHTS

I don't think Beethoven *wanted* to meet a guru
But this old friend of mine went off the deep end,
Walks around in orange robes, with his head shaved,
Wears sandals even in the snow (which is not real:
Only the Buddha in you is real),
And calls himself Swami. And he came to lunch,
       one day,
Ate only beans, drank only water,
And talked for two hours about holiness and spirit
      and essence
And non-being and so on and so forth.
Beethoven didn't talk much at all, not after the first
      five minutes,
But when the door closed behind that orange skirt
He exploded, "Herr Raffel, was *ist* das? A man—that?
What, I ask you, *what?*" I shrugged, not caring much
One way or the other: after all, I'd seen more swamis
In the last ten years than I'd seen real Christians.
"A man, yes," I said casually, and Beethoven got
      even angrier.
"Why does he *do* that to himself? And to us too, eh?
Does he think those verdamte beans are *holy?*
I felt like hitting him with the wine bottle—I did, I did!"
I shrugged again. "Might've done him some good,
      you know.
Maybe, if you got him just right, you could've knocked
      him smack into his next reincarnation.
You could've saved him all kinds of time."
Beethoven just sat staring at me, then abruptly smiled:
      "You're joking, Herr Raffel.
For a moment you frightened me."

15

Norteamericano, Sudamericano

"Canada?" he inquired on day, suddenly picking up on
      the word,
Which I had used many times before. He had simply
      never noticed.
"The country just to the north of us," I explained.
"It was a British colony, in your time. My wife grew
      up there,
Though she was born in the United States, she's an
      American citizen."
His huge eyebrows wrinkled painfully.
"American?" he asked quietly, and I could only smile
      and shrug and throw up my hands.
"One country at a time!" I laughed, getting up and
      walking to the phonograph,
(Which was already half worn out from singing to him
Almost day and night). "One country at a time.
How would you like to hear some Heitor Villa-Lobos?"
He crossed his big hands on his stomach, leaned back
      in the soft chair, and smiled.
"How lovely to have my ears back!" he murmured,
      closing his eyes.

DINING

It was not the restaurant which amazed him but the
      waitresses:
As the first one approached but didn't stop, swept past
      in a green haze,
I had the feeling that the small wooden table between
      us would soon be dancing,
As it were, on the point of a pin.
I felt muscles long out of use rippling like the
      Atlantic Ocean.
The waitress did not seem to notice anything, but then
      she was used to being on display
And I doubt that Beethoven could have meant
      much to her.
He was far too civilized, too constrained, too
      definitely a man of his own time
To say anything, even to me, but words were
      clearly unnecessary,
Unheard melodies were twice as sweet,
And I had no trouble reading the swirl and spin
      in his eyes.
As the waitress assigned to our table veered toward us
In her short tight skirt, and even tighter blouse
Under which she visibly wore nothing but herself,
I could see his lips part, I could see his tongue
Lolling out, like a Great Dane after a long run
Or a wolf getting its first up-wind whiff of deer
After a long cold winter in the woods.
"I'll have the salad plate," I said discreetly,
But Beethoven just stared straight ahead, I think for the
      moment quite unable to speak,
Her nipples exactly at eye level for him.

17

"And you, sir?" she said once more, pushing out her
        hip, annoyed, pencil poised, eyes narrowing.
"Ach, it all looks good to me," he finally managed, his
        voice a delightfully husky tenor,
"It all looks good to me."
Whereupon he closed the menu with a snap
And, perhaps in a last-ditch effort to save himself,
        closed his eyes.
"*Two* salad plates," I said hurriedly, and she left us.
"It's all right," I whispered carefully, so as not to
        embarrass him; I leaned
Across the little table and lightly touched him arm.
        "It's all right, she's gone."
He opened his eyes, smiled, then closed them again.
"For you, maybe," he said with a sigh, "but not for me."
I sat there as quietly as a mouse, until the food arrived:
Genius, after all, has its prerogatives.

18

Six Million

For a man who got more than his money's worth from
      television,
Who worked the phonograph as his ancestors had
      worked plough horses,
Beethoven surprised me by not much caring for movies.
"It's the crowds," he explained one sunny day, as we
      sat in the yard.
He would never sit on the front porch, where we
      could be watched.
"Stay around Germans too much, you know, and you
      become suspicious of crowds."
I smiled grimly back at him. "I have travelled a lot,
      Herr Beethoven,
I have lived in many countries. But though I
      speak German
I have never set foot in the country. I suspect I
      never will."
It was his turn to be surprised. "So?"
I sighed. "I'm Jewish, you know."
He blinked. "And?"
I frowned. "Hitler—and all that," I said a little roughly.
"Hitler?"

CRITICS

"Now that I hear them," Beethoven half whispered to
    me, one night,
When we had remedied history for the half-dozenth time
By playing him a superb recording of his
    Ninth Symphony,
"Now that I really and truly hear them, I admit the
    vocal writing is rather craggy,
Maybe even a little difficult." He smiled. "Herr Raffel,
Do you know how it hurts to admit that maybe the
    critics were right?"
Did I know!
"Difficult, shmifficult," I answered, "they've been
    managing for almost two hundred years.
Don't change a single note!"
He was startled. "Himmel! What an idea!
Did you think I would? After all this time? Never, I
    assure you: never."
And then I smiled too. "The difficult is good for us,
    Herr Beethoven,
Though the critics don't know it. They like the perverse,
Which is not at all the same thing."
He patted my hand and chuckled: "We have a hard
    time of it,
We artists, don't we?" I laughed with him
And then we drank to our pain and suffering
In amber Courvoisier brandy, V.S.O.

ALEXANDER GRAHAM BELLS

He liked the telephone. Now that his ears
      functioned again
There was nothing he liked better than a
      woman's voice—
Any woman, a long distance operator would do,
      though of course
There was no one left to call, long distance—and the
      new male operators
Saddened him—but all the same the telephone
      produced women's voices at the expense of
      nothing more elaborate than seven-digit dialing.
He would have liked to call all the women in the
      Denver phone book
But he settled for all the women in our address books,
      my wife and I.
Sometimes they talked to him, sometimes they didn't
(If a stranger started off with, "Hello! I'm Ludwig Van
      Beethoven,
What can I say to you today?"—I mean,
How many people, even knowing me, would keep on
      listening?),
But Beethoven was not much disturbed.
"It's the attempt that matters," he assured me. "One
      soprano sentence is enough
For a man like me. When you reach a certain age. . ."
But would it stay enough?
What if time did not work at all like saltpeter?
I was sorry, just then, that the telephone had ever
      been invented.

THE WILD WEST

"What is Cheyenne?" he asked one day, pointing to a
    green and white road sign
As we drove along to the supermarket. He had
    adjusted to modern traffic surprisingly quickly,
And I knew pretty soon, if he stayed, I would have to
    teach him how to drive. "Oh, I'm sorry!" I
    said hastily.
"We've been so busy—you know,
Taping your oral history and all that—
That I've totally neglected to show you the country
    around here.
It's beautiful, really it is. We must take a drive—
    maybe later today."
"No, Herr Raffel, it is all as it should be,
I quite understand, believe me."
The soft burr of Austrian German underlay his speech—
He was born in Holland, yes, but he'd lived most of
    his life in Vienna—
And his manners, contrary to the accounts I had read,
    were exquisite.
"But do tell me, please, what is Cheyenne?"
And I wished, turning into the parking lot
And shutting down the motor of my Ford station wagon,
That I could answer as simply as he had asked.

ENGORGING

Beethoven went nuts at the House of Pies:
He had a piece of French blackbottom
And then a piece of Boston cream
And then the coconut custard
And after that the pecan (à la mode, with two
        scoops of vanilla)
And then the Dutch apple
And he finished up with a bran muffin, two chocolate
        chip cookies,
A raspberry iced cupcake, and a slice of sour cream
        coffee cake (with whipped cream).
I watched, but I couldn't believe it
Until my wife smiled and assured me
That a hundred and fifty years of sweet tooth
Must be naturally explosive.

NEWS

It was not music which most pleased Beethoven,
But the daily newspaper. He would read it from front
      to back,
Sometimes more than once, trying to digest the
      indigestible,
Not only stock market reports, and grain prices, and
      insurance quotations,
But fires, burglaries, international conniving,
      fashion, editorials,
Even sports. "You don't know what a baseball is!" I
      swore, once,
For a moment impatient. "You don't know the
      difference between a bull market and a certified
      public accountant!
Do you know where Rhodesia *is?* Or Lebanon?
Who's the Prime Minister of France? What's a Soviet?"
He was not troubled. "But, Herr Raffel," he said simply,
"I know this"—and he touched his big square hand to
      his chest, just above his heart.

NEW YORK

He wanted me to take him to New York City.
He wanted to see the Empire State Building and
       Central Park and the Statue of Liberty,
He wanted to go to the Metropolitan Museum and the
       opera, and the New York Philharmonic, and the
       Museum of Modern Art,
He wanted to take the ferry to Staten Island and drive
       across the George Washington Bridge,
He wanted to ride every subway everywhere, and
       shop at Macy's, and eat whole wheat doughnuts
       at Chock Full O'Nuts,
And go to the zoo, and walk down Fifth Avenue, and
       down the Boardwalk at Coney Island,
He wanted to try everything at Steeplechase Park, he
       wanted to spend a Sunday afternoon at the
       Cloisters,
He wanted to kiss the mayor and address the city council,
He wanted to conduct the Edwin Franko Goldman
       Band in Sousa marches on a starry
       night in Prospect Park,
He wanted to go to the latest movie, he wanted to
       see the ballet at Lincoln Center,
He wanted to give advice to the Ford Foundation and
       happiness to Harlem,
He wanted to play a concert at Carnegie Hall and one
       at Town Hall, and he wanted to hug
       Leonard Bernstein.
Oh, he wanted, he wanted!

But how could I do it to him, how could I willingly
    expose him to that stinking urban slime?
He only knew the words, he only knew the history: I
    knew what was what.
"It's all on me," he cajoled, "I'll pay for everything!"
But I just shook my head:
"Not if you *gave* me the place, Beethoven. And I'll tell
    the State Department you're in the country
    illegally
If you try to go on your own. You stay away from
    New York City, do you hear?"
He was a man about it, he did not weep, but he was
    badly disappointed.
"Maybe Chicago?" he bargained. "Dallas? Detroit?
    Los Angeles?"
We finally settled for San Francisco: after all, I couldn't
    just keep saying no to him.

OTITIS

When my niece—a professional interpreter
For the deaf—heard that Beethoven was in Denver,
And in my house, she called to tell me that the challenge
Really appealed to her. "Words are one thing,"
          she explained,
"But music—wow!" I think she was disappointed,
Learning that he'd recovered his hearing
In time. But she's a realistic young lady
And wished him luck. "Amy," I said,
"The next time he goes deaf I'll have him see you,
I'll give him your card, I know he'll be grateful,
You just wait." I'm not sure she was much impressed
But all the same she promised to visit Denver,
Though perhaps only after Beethoven had moved on.

Disguises

There are not many places Beethoven would have
       been unwelcome
If they knew who he was. But when they knew
They would usually refuse to believe.
So I generally didn't tell them,
I let him appear to be a perfectly ordinary
       American citizen
Who happened to like ruffled silk shirts and
       heavy-brimmed top hats and calfskin gloves
And laced Empire boots and morning coats with
       velvet lapels
And pantaloons of a sort no American outside a movie
       studio has seen since
       John Quincy Adams and Andrew Jackson—
A perfectly inconspicuous American who swore
       under his breath
In German, and conducted invisible orchestras with
       his left hand
While humming three-part harmonies and carrying
       on a heated conversation
About God and Civilization and the Nine Muses
       from Olympos
Who walk the earth in human guise, and with whom
He is in fairly constant telepathic communication.
The results of these subtle disguises were frequently
       of real interest
Though not always amusing.

CAREER COUNSELING

"Beethoven," I said to him one rainy day, when he
        could not walk
His usual fifteen miles between breakfast and lunch;
The rain had just stopped, but it was dark and
        threatening and rather cool,
"Beethoven, don't you intend to make anything
        of yourself?
Don't you want to get a job, settle down, maybe
        get married,
Raise a family? You're getting lazy, you know: all
        this walking
Is just an excuse for never getting anything done.
        You're not bringing yourself to bear on yourself
The way you used to do. Time is slipping away on
        you, and you don't seem to notice it going by—
You haven't even written a note since you've been
        back, and you've been back,
You know, kind of a long time. Isn't it time you got a
        move on?"
I kept my voice soft, I tried not to seem too paternal,
I didn't want to lecture him, all I wanted
Was to jostle him a little, make him consider a
        few basic verities.
If he had had the walking stick he used to carry,
        back in the old days
In Vienna, I think he might have knocked me down:
As it was, he cursed—very loudly—for a good
        three minutes,
Kicked rather a lot of grass loose, and some dirt with
        it—we were standing on the front lawn,

Under the weeping birch I had planted four years ago
When we moved to Denver—and consistently avoided
        looking at me, face to face.
I stayed calm, I remained patient, and when he
        finished scuffling and swearing
I decided to change the subject. "Would you care for
        an ice cream cone?"
I asked suavely, and he smiled. "Do they have
        chocolate fudge, Herr Raffel?"
"Oh, I think that might be arranged, Herr Beethoven!"

THE EQUAL RIGHTS AMENDMENT

"There are some things that do not change,"
        Beethoven said to my wife one night,
While the girls were clearing the table and we
        were finishing our wine,
"And one of those things, Gott sei danken! is women."
She sipped her wine. I had prepared the dinner,
        of course,
And done the grocery shopping that day, and run
        two loads of laundry,
And driven my daughters to the stationery shop
        for school supplies. My wife
Worked out of the house and I in it,
Which I imagine explains everything. "Is that so,
        Herr Beethoven?" she replied sweetly.
"Do tell us more." He cleared his throat, blushed, and
        tried to get his moorings—
He may be an old-fashioned sort, but he remains
        powerfully sensitive—
While she smiled on and on and he visibly wilted.
"Well," he said carefully, after a long silence, "it is
        also true that some things are exceedingly
Subtle, and therefore difficult to pin down in words."
She raised her glass in a wordless toast and he
        coughed and joined her,
And I quickly brought up the subject of desert:
I had prepared a chocolate mousse he was bound
        to enjoy,
I knew his weakness for everything chocolate.

THEY ALSO SERVE

"They pay you so much—for *teaching?*" Beethoven
      asked.
"Universities are a big business, these days," I assured
      him after noting
That it was not really so much that they paid me, not
      so much at all.
"The world of education is not what it was: time
      marches on!"
He sighed and drank some beer. "In my Vienna,
      Herr Raffel,
Teaching was much more a matter of public relations—
      of what you call advertising today—
Than a real source of income. And what dunderhead
      pupils I had!
You are fortunate, more even than you know."
I wanted to insist that I worked for my keep, but
      instead I commented that, somehow,
The Beethovens of the world seemed always to
      manage—but the Raffels, you know,
Well, *we* had to scramble. "And after all," I concluded
      with a flourish,
"How many Beethovens *are* there?" He blinked and
      stared hard at me:
I had not noticed, before, how exceedingly blue his
      eyes could become.
"And how many Raffels are there?" he demanded
      bluntly—
And with such plain intent that I could not answer,
I could only look down and wish that somehow I had
      managed, just this once, to keep my
      mouth shut.

PREMONITIONS

"Wagner is indeed the key," he sighed one day.
"He sits on my shoulders, all right, he renews
        everything."
I smiled, a little puzzled.
"But why does that make you unhappy, Herr Beethoven?"
He blew his nose, carefully, lengthily.
"A key opens things, Herr Raffel.
Suppose this turns out to be a Pandora's Box, eh?
Suppose, just suppose, I want to leave well
        enough alone?"
I crossed my legs and for a moment could not speak:
In Vienna, Beethoven had gone through locked doors—
Through stone walls, damn it, when they got in his way.
But—I consoled myself—after a hundred and fifty
        years he was tired,
Surely he was tired. "Are you tired?" I asked.
He sighed yet again.
"I'm concerned, Herr Raffel. That's all. Concerned."

UPROAR

"Wouldn't you like to try an opera, even?" I asked him
      one morning.
"I mean, the one you did write—the only one, of
      course: everyone knows that—
Cost you so much time, and worry, and in the end it
      didn't exactly turn out—well,
You know." He had never before looked at me quite
      so coldly.
"Do you not like my *Fidelio*?" he asked flatly, his eyes icy.
I tried to laugh it off. "It's not exactly a raving success,
Now is it? I mean, sure, there's great stuff in it,
There couldn't help but be great stuff in anything
      you wrote,
But when you come right down to it, after all, it isn't
      Mozart, is it?"
He glared. "And did you think it was meant to be?"
I decided that opera had become a dangerous subject.
"They say you had a green thumb, Herr Beethoven.
Let me show you my lilacs. And the irises. Please."

MEDICINALS

Beethoven did not like doctors. He had a painful
    shoulder
And I wanted him to get it treated, but he
    stubbornly refused to go,
Not after the still more painful experiences he had
    had with doctors,
Back in his own time. "Ach, such a mess they made
    of me, Herr Raffel!
And for what? For nothing, that's for what.
They helped me not one bit, for all the pain."
I tried to explain how much the medical profession
    had progressed,
What wonderful new methods they had evolved,
    what miraculous new drugs,
How much more scientific and therefore sensible it
    had all become.
I explained and explained and finally—he was as I
    have said truly a man of courage—
He agreed to make the experiment.
We drove to the office of a shoulder specialist,
    recommended by my own doctor,
And of course the first thing we had to do was fill
    out forms:
Beethoven took one look at the forms and
    handed them to me,
And of course I filled them out with all the required
    numbers and names and dates,
Especially insurance names and numbers.
But after we had waited one hour and fifty-seven
    minutes to be admitted to the examining rooms
The first thing the doctor did was to fill out forms

Of his own. "Have you been to a doctor in the last
        three years?" was his first question,
In a toneless voice that reminded me of computer
        simulated monsters in science fiction films.
"More like a hundred and fifty," Beethoven answered,
        cleverly adopting the same droning monotone,
"A hundred and fifty-two, to be exact." "I see,
And what was the name of the doctor who
        treated you on that occasion?" he asked.
Beethoven told him. He wrote it down. "And what
        was his address, please?"
Beethoven told him. He wrote it down. "And his
        telephone number, please?"
"He had no telephone," Beethoven said bluntly, in
        something like his normal voice.
The doctor hesitated, adjusted his glasses, coughed.
        "I see," he said a little more slowly.
"And was this a *rural* practice, Mr. Beethoven?" He
        pronounced it beet-hoven,
Like the vegetable. Beethoven stood up, and I
        stood up too, crestfallen in the extreme.
This had after all been entirely my idea. And
        now look what was happening!
"Good day, Herr Doktor," Beethoven said politely,
        tipping his hat.
The doctor blinked and put down his forms. He was
        smiling, after a fashion.
"Now!" he exclaimed with what was meant to be
        hearty good cheer, but emerged a bland
        baby talk,
"That wasn't exactly painful, was it?"
Beethoven opened first one door and then another,
        and we walked out without another word.

"Do you *see?*" he asked quite mildly, under all the
    circumstances,
As we snapped on the seat belts in my station wagon
    and prepared to drive home.
"I see," I admitted sadly.
"I can perhaps try hot water," Beethoven mused,
    flexing his aching shoulder.
"Hot water is usually safe." I agreed. It had definitely
    been my experience
That under most conditions hot water was safe, in
    moderation to be sure.
The telephone was ringing inside the house, as we
    walked up the driveway,
But I suspected it was the receptionist at the shoulder
    doctor's office
And since we had no intention of speaking to her or
    to her doctor, this afternoon
Or any afternoon in any foreseeable future, we did
    not hurry
And the telephone was obliging enough to have
    become silent even before I got my key in the
    front door and the front door open.
I held the door for Beethoven and made an elaborate
    and deferential gesture.
"After you, cher Ludwig!" I said, and he laughed and
    quite as obliging as the telephone,
Walked in. Without a word we headed directly for
    the kitchen,
Where we cracked a few beers, and ate some excellent
    Dutch cheese
On equally excellent American crackers,
And by that time Beethoven's shoulder was feeling
    no pain
And there was no need even for hot water, even
    in moderation.

"But of course," I explained, suddenly remembering
      that I'd never told him,
"Wagner started off by imitating *you*. Real imitations,
      piano sonatas, symphonies,
The works." He smiled tolerantly. "But of course,
      Herr Raffel."
"I mean," I added hastily, "I don't want you to think
      even Wagner
Could ignore you." "Ach, natürlich. But tell me:
Does it bother you, this imitation? It seems that
      perhaps it does. It should not,
You should never be ashamed of learning from
      Goethe, of imitating Schiller—
Schiller!—or of copying, here and there,
From Hölderin, or Lessing, even from old Hans Sachs.
      Didn't I ape Haydn,
Even Mozart, once upon a time?"
I cleared my throat: as a musicological lecturer
Plainly I was a good house painter. "Try Shakespeare,"
      I suggested.
"Shakespeare? Shakespeare? Yes, of course!" He
      laughed.
"Is that who you imitate, Herr Raffel, when you
      write poetry?"
I was doing no better, even as a literary pedagogue.
"Do you play tennis?" I wondered.

RETROSPECTION

I wish Beethoven had come sooner:
I could have used his help, twenty years ago,
When I was practicing law on Wall Street.
He would have cut right through the bullshit, he
      would have separated
Staves from music, ends from means, with a flick of
      the wrist.
"You are too fond of music, for a non-musician,"
      he told me one day.
"No one should spend so much time with what he
      does not fully understand.
Love has nothing to do with it: you delude yourself,
      Herr Raffel."
Another time, as I came home from the university,
      very tired, very very tired,
He took my briefcase out of my hand and told me
      not to let students—
Even graduate students, whose need is greatest of all—
      trouble me as they did:
"You must not let them feed on your insides," he
      smiled fiercely.
Prometheus is Prometheus, and you are Raffel."
I could not argue with him; even if I had not been
      tired I could not have argued.
I just wish I could have introduced my first wife to
      him, before I married her,
And also the second.
I wonder if he would have let me take a Ph.D.?

SNOW

Colorado snow, according to Beethoven,
Was basically lunatic. "There's far too much of it,
      for one thing,"
He informed me, reflecting back on his first
      American winter,
"And it stays on the ground too long, and it lies
      too deep—
It's ridiculous! Even in Switzerland they clean the
      streets better."
I agreed, of course, but went on to explain that snow,
Like earthquakes and vanity and hurricanes and
      politicians
Was a natural disaster and best accepted, not
      fought against.
"You learn to live with it," I told him, as we laced
      on our boots
And clomped out into the yard. I threw my first
      snowball of the spring
Over the side of the house, then banged one into
      a tree, and another on the back gate,
Still another into the garage wall, and finally,
When Beethoven stooped to pack himself a snowball,
I hit him too. He threw at me, but clumsily,
      and missed,
So I taught him the finer points of the art. He
      laughed and continued to miss,
And the dogs wrestled and barked in the drifts, and
      we stomped and shouted
For nearly an hour. Over a cup of hot tea

(Which he laced with rum: he'd grown quite fond
          of rum, which they had not enjoyed
Back in Vienna) he assured me that, for a natural disaster,
Snow really wasn't so bad after all.
"Better than politicians?" I grinned at him,
And he nodded most emphatically. "Yes!" he
          exclaimed, thumping the table.
"What could be worse than politicians, eh?"
I realized that he was becoming Americanized.

DOGS

Beethoven liked dogs, and not just for their soft
        thick fur.
He like watching them, comparing their games,
        their tricks,
To human ones. He liked talking to them, too:
Their responses, he insisted, were indicative of
        truly fundamental things.
"A dog goes straight to the heart of it!" he roared
        one afternoon,
Fresh from a roll on the floor with all three of them.
        "A dog lives too fully, too much in the
        here-and-now,
To be petty—or pompous—or pretentious—none
        of that!" He wiped his sweating face
With a red handkerchief—he was partial to red—
And thanked me for the iced tea I'd made him.
"Your dogs would be stupendous orchestral musicians,"
        he assured me,
"Full of ensemble spirit. They have that marvelous
        pack sense
Which violinists, especially, can't seem ever to acquire.
Why are violinists so selfish, eh?" he demanded,
And I smiled and told him I'd been a violinist,
        more or less,
From age six to age seven. "Ah, it did not affect you,
        Herr Raffel!
Definitely, you are more like a dog!"
I felt reasonably sure that I was being complimented.

SAWDUST

There were always problems—naturally. Who wants
        to talk about problems
When you can talk about Beethoven?
But whether you talk about them or not they stay
        the same,
They're still there. And there were problems with
        Beethoven.
We had no piano: that was problem number one.
He could not understand how we could have two
        cars—two!—
And no piano. "Ten, fifteen thousand dollars they
        cost, right?
And you try to tell me you can't afford a *piano?*
        Ach, nein, das ist *letterlich*, Herr Raffel,
        ganz letterlich!"
How do you tell Beethoven you can't ride a piano
        to the supermarket?
It was ridiculous, maybe, as he said it was,
But it was also a problem.
And too many of my German books were
        translations: he didn't want *translations,*
He wanted *books!* I explained that I read English more
        readily than I did German
And that they were good translations and that lots of
        translations were better than lots of originals
And that anyway I was myself a translator. It
        didn't matter:
"Reading a translation, Herr Raffel, is like playing a
        sonata on a dummy keyboard.

43

You know the thing I mean?" I nodded: "You
          practice on it, it makes no sound."
"Exactly! That is what reading a German book in
          translation is like, exactly that!
Tell me, would you eat bread if it were baked
          with *sawdust* instead of flour?"
He was triumphant, but I could not help laughing.
"People do," I told him. "Real sawdust. They call
          it bulk. Honest, I'm not kidding."
He just stared at me, his lips working,
Then turned away and stood at the window,
          silently, for a solid quarter of an hour.

SOCIAL SECURITY

"You'll need a Social Security card," I told him
      one morning.
His face was blank. "I mean," I went on, "if you
      get a job
Or teach or anything like that." He frowned: "Social
      Security?"
I offered him more coffee but he waved it away.
"It's like a kind of national insurance," I tried to explain.
"They take a certain amount out of your salary and
      when you're old enough,
Like sixty-five, usually, they pay it back to you."
His eyes had darkened.
"They?" was all he said, and I had to explain that yes,
      I meant the government.
He did not ask what *that* meant, we both knew
      perfectly well.
"And they give it *all* back to you?" he finally said,
      spreading both hands on the table in front of him.
"Well, no," I admitted—what else could I do? Lie
      to him?—
"They give you a check every month, just a small
      amount, really,
But if you live long enough you get a lot of money.
      You do, really."
He nodded grimly. "A check? Paper money they
      give you?
Ach, that is a government, that is how they have
      always done it!"
There was nothing else I could say.

CUISINE À L'AMÉRICAIN

"Would you like a malted?" I asked Beethoven one
        hot afternoon.
He did not know what I was talking abut. I explained.
"Ice cream?" "Crême glacée," I told him, more or
        less accurately.
"And *milk*?" His nose seemed to curl. "Also honey,"
        I added,
"And a ripe banana, and malted powder, and
        sometimes wheat germ
And always a raw egg or two." He blanched but
        agreed to taste.
He tasted, spat, and asked for red wine to wash out
        his mouth.
"Is this how you conquered the West?" he inquired wryly.
"I can see, now, how you defeated both the Germans
        and the Japanese:
No civilized man could drink that, Herr Raffel,
        and survive.
It is a drink of barbarian power."
I drank mine, and then his, and then refilled my glass
With what was left in the blender.
"Chacun á son gout, cher Ludwig," I smiled.
"We not only won the West, but we've kept it—and
        don't forget, please,
That right at this minute you yourself are *in* it. Cheers!"
I emptied it down, patted my stomach, and proposed
        a walk.
Beethoven was unusually silent:
Plainly, though I had given him very little to drink
I had given him rather a lot to think about.

Early to Rise

It wasn't exactly that Beethoven ate too much:
He'd never been a fat man, not even in Vienna,
        exposed to all those fragrant pastry shops
And the thick cream and free flowing beer—not to
        mention chocolate.
He'd always burned up what he ate, and he'd always
        worked too hard
And moved too fast to get fat. But then was then
And now was now and if he wasn't getting fat
He certainly wasn't getting any thinner.
"Would you like to try an exercise program?" I asked
        him on Sunday,
After he'd put in three hours watching an opera, an
        hour and a half taking in a ballet,
And two one-hour stretches with the Boston and
        Chicago orchestras
(He made good use of television, you have to give
        him that).
"A who?" he asked, chuckling, and I tried to explain.
"Ho-ho," he laughed, "I'll do even better than that,
        I'll chop all your wood for you.
I'm a very handy man with an axe."
I made a deferential gesture: "We don't burn wood
        any more. It's all gas from a pipe."
"All right," he said at once. "I'll do all the family
        washing. How's that?
My mother did all the washing once upon a time:
Am I any better than my mother?"
I cleared my throat:

"We have a washing machine. And a dryer. And,"
        I added,
Just to make the list complete, "we have a
        dish-washing machine too."
He wet his lips and stopped smiling.
"I have decided to get fat," he announced.

AKADEMIA

I tried to introduce Beethoven to my colleagues—
        professional men,
Well educated, some of them deeply found of music,
        some of them still fond of books—
But they could not understand him, his assertions
        about music were terribly absolute
(And had no footnotes), he invariably drove them
        away, they would start to twitch as he spoke
And then they would flee. Beethoven felt the same
        about them:
"Dried-up apples," he said wrinkling his nose
        (which was larger than the pictures made it out
        to be,
And fleshier also: I was very surprised, at first).
        "Good in fruit soup—cooked, boiled,
Spiced, with good fresh bread and cheese. Strong
        cheese. But by themselves?
Garnicht! Nothing!"
I am not myself very fond of dried apples, so I did not
        come to their defense:
We played a game of chess, instead, and it satisfied
        all our need for impartial logic.

49

MARRIAGE

Beethoven could not understand my wife's friends,
        handsome women, lively, bright,
Well-spoken, warm: "They're none of them married,
        Herr Raffel!
What has happened to all these people? Where will
        you find tomorrow
Without today?" I refilled his glass:
He was growing very accustomed to the cheap
        California wine
I drank out of habit and fiscal necessity.
"You see," I sighed, not sure I really could explain
        anything, "it *is* very different, now.
Women don't rush into marriage, the way they used
        to. They have other things to do.
And then—well, it's a little like buying fresh fruit in
        the market.
They want a nibble here and a nibble there,
        before they buy.
They want to squeeze the oranges and poke the bananas,
They don't want what we call premature involvement—
        which they think of, I suppose,
As a kind of legal indigestion." He scowled.
"But you were never married, Beethoven!" I
        added quickly,
"Who are you to talk?"
He threw back his head and laughed.
"Who better, eh? Who better?"

CONCERT

I hesitated about exposing Beethoven to "live" music;
    there were so many risks.
But finally, last night, we decided to take the chance,
And the three of us drove down to Denver's lovely
    new concert hall,
Built in the round, recently opened, expensive,
    tactfully modern:
Its acoustics had received rave reviews, critics had
    flown in from all around the country to hear for
    themselves.
Beethoven liked it even before a note had been played:
"Grand," he said, sitting in the plain wooden chairs,
    "but not *too* grand.
Simple. Very nice, yes. What do you call that stuff again?"
"Concrete." "Ach: lovely. Such nice textures, very
    good for music, I can tell already.
Who do you say is playing?" "The greatest flautist
    of our day,"
I told him with some pleasure, "Jean Pierre Rampal."
He chuckled: "The French and their flutes! So it has
    not changed.
And what is he playing, the great Frenchman?"
I showed him a program, and he studied it with great
    care, then grunted.
He had a virtuosic grunt, and I did not know what this
    one was intended to convey,
And I did not want to find out before I had to. I had
    always had secret visions
Of Beethoven leaping up, at a concert, and running to
    the stage to embrace the musicians

51

And lecture the conductor and preach the eternal
    virtues of freedom and his own music.
How would I get him out of it, if he did that? And
    wouldn't they try to lock me up too
If I told them who he was, if I seemed to live in what
    they would see as his deluded fantasy?
Would even the musicians believe him? What would
    Jean Pierre Rampal say,
What would he do, elegant Parisian though he was,
    man of the world, sophisticate,
Scholar and teacher? What would I do, in his place? I
    hunched down in my chair and waited.
There were no fireworks. The first piece on the
    program, a Mozart sonata, was predictably
    impeccable:
Rampal danced quietly as he played, and the music
    rippled and shone.
"A violin piece, no?" Beethoven said rather sourly.
    "He is a flautist, no?"
The Schubert *Arpeggione* sonata followed—so
    romantically unlike the Mozart
That Rampal had to stand silently tensing himself, for
    some moments, before he could begin.
"Ja. Franz always liked those crazy instruments.
    Arpeggione! Letterlich!
The cello was good enough for me, you know. I did
    not need novelty to say what I had to say.
Never!" He said nothing of the performance, so
    moving that a single fluffed note
In a mad cluster meant to be articulated with a bow
    and four main strings
Stood out, but did not matter in the least.

And then, of the Kuhlau work that brought us to
 the intermission,
Beethoven said brusquely, dismissively: "Technical.
 Imitative. I could do that with my left hand."
Something was bothering him, and I did not know
 what. My wife suggested a glass of wine
And he declined: whatever was wrong was badly wrong!
It was a gorgeous recital, but I was almost sorry we
 had come.
Should we leave? Beethoven sensed the suggestion:
"Time for more," he said doggedly, as though it was
 something to be endured.
We made our way back to our seats: There were
 thousands of people,
Rampal's reputation had filled the hall.
"Stupendous!" I muttered involuntarily, after the first
 movement of the Franck A Minor,
Written for violin: Beethoven had heard it, and liked
 it, on my phonograph.
But he pretended not to hear me, sat stiffly, glumly
 attentive. He was listening,
All right—but what was he hearing?
The final piece on the printed program was a clever
 contraption of runs and grace notes,
Arpeggios and trills: Rampal blew it like a Technicolor
 kaleidoscope,
The audience murmured its appreciation even before
 he ran it to the end.
But Beethoven sat and glowered: he was not keen
 on virtuosic display, everyone knew that.
Neither did he join in the massive applause, the
 shouts of "bravo, bravo!"

That led Rampal to give us no less than four encores,
        a melting Chopin,
A briskly charming Von Weber, an American bit of pop
        trivia and finally
A jazz-influenced thing by Claude Bolling that he
        danced through as deftly, as beautifully,
As anything and everything he played. Beethoven
        never applauded:
Had that been his habit, in Vienna? I did not believe it.
I was almost discouraged: could we try a second
        concert, after a start like this?
"Herr Beethoven," I forced myself to say, as we drove
        home, "do you dislike the flute?"
"Splendid instrument," he muttered. "And Monsieur
        Rampal?"
"Splendid, admirable, yes," he muttered again.
I tried to understand. "But you didn't enjoy the
        concert," I noted.
"That was all too clear. Should we not have gone?"
His fist hit out at the padded inside of the door; it
        was so loud, so vicious, so sudden
        and unexpected
That I nearly drove us off the road.
"Gott verdamte. . ." He went on, expletive
        after expletive,
For several minutes, then sat in red-faced,
        panting silence. Neither my wife nor I
Spoke, the rest of the way. I could not understand,
        not any of it.
But just before we reached our house I had to speak up.
"Herr Beethoven," I began with considerable hesitation,
        but he cut me off instantly.

"Herr Beethoven! Exactly! Herr Beethoven—and
    where was he on that so-called program, eh?
This is your greatest flautist and he plays a full
    program and seventeen dozen encores
And never plays one single verdamte note written
    by Herr Beethoven! This is a great musician or
    a fluter-tooter, eh?
This is what you call an evening of *music*? Gott
    verdamte. . ."—and this time he cursed for only
Ten or twelve seconds. I could see his teeth grinding.
    I tried not to smile.
As I parked the car I assured him, quietly but earnestly
    too, that I would write to Monsieur Rampal,
I would explain the situation to him, and I was
    sure—but Beethoven cut me off once again.
"*You* will write to him, Herr Raffel? Nein! *I* will write
    to that nose-snuffing Frenchman,
I will tell him—ach, how I will tell him!"
By the time we walked into the house he was in an
    expansive, delighted mood,
And after my wife had excused herself and gone
    up to bed
We sat in the kitchen until three, swapping jokes.

EXPLORATION

We took him for a drive, my wife and I,
And he was ecstatic, he had never seen anything like
       it, not even in the Alps—
"They are bigger indeed, Herr Raffel: you were right!"—
And every great rock face, every sweeping panorama,
       every huge stand of pine trees,
Running for miles up steep slopes, made him gasp
       and splutter.
"Beautiful, beautiful, beautiful,
So very beautiful!" But the thin clear mountain stream
       we pulled up beside,
So he could see the shallow water pounding downhill,
       so he could hear its roar,
Totally silenced him. He did not speak for nearly
       an hour,
After we'd started up again.
"He is still in the world," he finally said, just barely loud
       enough so we could hear him.
"I had thought perhaps He was gone, but He is not,
       He is still here."
I was driving a difficult stretch of road and not
       concentrating.
"Who?" I asked, not turning around.

Paralytic Philosophy

It wasn't that Beethoven disliked machines, he generally
Ignored them: results had always been his forte,
He did what needed to be done, it was—and he knew
      it—his secret weapon,
Then and now. "You think too much, Herr Raffel,"
He told me many times. "That which is thought is not
      accomplished:
Indeed, thinking prevents action, nicht wahr?"
I had thought the same thing so many times
That I hesitated: to agree with him as enthusiastically
      as I would have had to
Might seem slavish, while to disagree would be
      hypocritical.
In the meantime, he opened another beer,
Looked happily around at the budding trees and the
      grass going green,
And exclaimed: "Ach, wie wunderbar ist der Frühling!"
And then of course I had to agree: spring was indeed
      wonderful.
And what would he do, I immediately wondered, if
      he'd reappeared where German was not spoken?
And then I realized that I was—once again—thinking
      too much
And also that he had already changed the subject
And—finally—that spring was in truth a great deal
      more interesting
Than anything inside my head.

BEATLEMANIA

One of my writing students—a poet—
Dropped by one afternoon, score in hand,
To discuss the orchestration of the *Eroica Symphony.*
Beethoven was polite but bored: the *Eroica*, after all,
       was by now a hundred and seventy years old
And he had other things cooking.
My student, who had done time in a conservatory on
       the East Coast
And still played the flute like a demon,
Pressed on, more or less diplomatically, but
       increasingly uphill.
She could not understand. And I decided not to
       intervene:
Wasn't this too a part of education? Wouldn't I be
       depriving her of something important
If I stepped in? "Fraulein," Beethoven suddenly said,
       in his best and most gentlemanly manner,
Simultaneously bouncing out of his chair,
"If I can persuade Herr Professor Doktor Raffel here
To put a Beatles record on his excellent phonograph,
Will you show me how you dance to it?"
A minute later he was wriggling and smiling
       (she was an excellent dancer)
And studying the aerodynamical configurations which
       first-class rock and roll
Induced under her blouse.

CAVEAT MUSICUS

Orchestras were better now, Beethoven told me:
    better trained,
Better paid, better fed, better conducted. "But such
    short programs!" he marveled.
"You know, Herr Raffel, in my time a concert would
    be three hours, maybe more.
We would do maybe a symphony, to start, then a
    concerto, and an overture or two,
And then another symphony, and another concerto,
    even for a different instrument,
And finish off with a long choral piece. And repeat
    one of the symphonies as an encore.
And now! You do maybe two symphonies, with an
    intermission in between—
And poof! It's all over, everyone goes home. Well,
    it changes,
It changes: it's all for the best. But then," he couldn't
    help adding,
"Half the musicians are women." He shook his head,
    frowning. "Women!
I tell you, *that* is something I will never understand.
    Never."
I didn't ask him what he had against women: I knew.
"They're half the human race," I noted as mildly as
    I could.
"And the better half!" he replied at once. "Much too
    good for public appearances
Sawing on celli and banging on drums!" I laughed,
    how could I help laughing?
"I'll bet you're against abortion too, Herr Beethoven!"

He blinked, genuinely confused. "Abortion?"
I made him a liverwurst sandwich on dark
       pumpernickel bread
And spread the butter just as thick as he liked it
       (half an inch):
After all I could not expect too much of him,
I had to be reasonable,
Like his Viennese audiences I had to learn to like
       what he gave me.

Collaborations

My good friend Francis Sullivan, a jolly Jesuit
And the best religious poet now writing in English,
Unexpectedly flew in to Denver one night. It was not
       a problem:
He was glad to see Beethoven, though he hadn't
       known my other friend was here,
And by letting both my daughters sleep downstairs,
       giving both their rooms to our guests,
It all worked out. Francis had called after Beethoven
       was in bed,
So the two of them slept, that one night, door-to-door,
       without yet having met.
And in the morning they were both up with the sun,
Both cheerful, hungry—as ever—for coffee and
       conversation.
"Tell me, Herr Beethoven," Francis asked over
       buttered toast,
"How do we strike you, as a people? Do we
       seem ignorant
Of the spirit, as so many people today think we do?"
Beethoven stirred more sugar into his coffee,
His sweet tooth insatiable. He put a thick slap of
       jelly on his toast.
He cleared his throat and considered the thick varnish
       I'd put on the dining room table,
Which I built myself: he was immensely found of
       that table.
"Spirit, Father Sullivan," he finally answered, carefully
       moderating his voice,

"Spirit is something that I, in my ignorance, somehow
        find everywhere, in everyone,
And I can see no difference between now and then.
        Man is man.
And God is God. And we coexist forever, as we
        always must,
As we always have. Only the forms change—and
        what are forms?"
Francis raised both arms high, as if intoning a blessing,
And laughed with delight. "Eureka!" he cried. "A man
        after my own heart!"
Beethoven looked at him, slightly dubious: there was
        after all the backwards collar
(Even though Francis was not at the moment wearing it)
And all those years of rigid clericalism. But he knew
        that his ears had not deceived him,
He knew that he had indeed heard what he'd heard.
"Tell me, Father," he wondered, still a little cautious, but
        believing more and more every moment,
"Do you ever write texts for choral settings?"
For a minute I thought Francis would do a dance
        around the dining room.
"Do I ever. . .do I *ever*!" he bubbled,
And then I was sure he'd throw his arms around
        Beethoven.
But he quietly refolded his disarranged napkin.
"May I call you Ludwig?" he asked sedately.
(No one but Francis can seem to dance, without every
        actually rising from his chair.
It is a unique gift.) Beethoven smiled and nodded.
"Listen, Ludwig," Francis started to explain, his eyes
        round and warm,
"I believe in bringing *everything* I can to the pulpit,

Poetry, music, the dance—everything! For years, now,
I've wanted. . ." And Beethoven did indeed listen,
His eyes too began to glow and without his knowing it
His right hand began to tap out rhythms, I could even
      see his chest rising and falling
As he started to sing silently, deep inside himself.
And I envied Francis his directness, his zeal, and
      almost most of all
The courage which had immediately put him on
      first-name terms with the greatest musician
Of any time, then or now. I'd wanted to call Ludwig
      by his first name;
I'd wanted to have him set my poems to music—
      oh Lord!
Francis flew in, overnight, and it all happened: he
      flew in and truly, fully,
He arrived, he was *there*. Neither of them would
      let it drop, now,
They would *do* it, they wouldn't let it fade away in
      bright-eyed talk.
And even as I loved them both, I envied them both,
And wished that I could be like either one of them,
Knowing as I wished it that I was being (as usual)
      foolish,
But also knowing that, forever and forever, I was
      as I was,
And I was not as I was not.

DISPLACEMENTS

He had not liked being born Dutch:
Beethoven freely admitted his own prejudice.
"Well, it might have been pleasant, you know," he
       reflected one sunny afternoon,
"To have been born French. Yes. But then, only the
       French can truly understand other Frenchmen!"
His smile was unusually mellow.
"Germany produces great artists—still," I smiled back,
And he straightened, scowling. Beethoven's scowl was
       monumental, it was all that the picture of him
       had said it was.
"I am not German!" he barked. "I speak the language,
I like the food. But Herr Raffel, do not deceive
       yourself, I am *not* German!"
"Viennese," I corrected myself quickly. He laughed.
"Much better, much better. But in truth I was not Dutch
Or French or German or even Viennese. No. I was
       European. I was."
He sat staring at the fence, his face expressionless.
"And now?" I wondered carefully.
He shrugged, very slowly, then put his hands behind
       his neck,
Tilted back his head, and stared up at the sky. It was
       blue and cloudless,
It was bright and it was hot, and there was nothing
       to see.
"And now?" he repeated heavily. "Now? What am I,
       eh? A good question.
A displacement? A time-freak? Am I indeed really and
       truly here?

Am I?" "I see you," I assured him,
"I speak to you, others speak to you, you answer."
He got up and walked back and forth, his hands
        behind his back, now,
His shoes digging holes in the grass.
"And does that signify, eh? Does that prove anything?"
He stalked up and down, his feet pounding even
        through the thick grass—
Until, suddenly, I laughed.
"Does anything prove anything, my dear Beethoven?
Are you even sure of your name?"
He stopped, but his smile did not return.
"No, no, I'm not. It's true. I never *was* sure,
        you know.
And still I'm not. Still!" he shook his head.
"What's wrong with us, eh, Herr Raffel?
Are we all really so desperately unsure as we seem?
Has humanity ever put one single foot in front of
        another foot
And truly been sure it would touch the ground?
What's wrong with us?" But my smile refused to fade.
"How odd," I said to him quietly. "You almost sound
        like me
Complaining about me!" He stood looking back at me.
"Odd," he murmured, as if testing the word—then
        threw back his head,
Roared with laughter, stamped his feet and roared and
        stamped some more.
"What's odd about it, eh, Raffel? We've lived together
        for months and months,
I dropped down on you out of the past. Why,
We're almost like an old married couple! Odd?

No! Of course we've come to resemble each other!"
"Lord!" I protested. "You should have rubbed off on me,
Not me on you." He chuckled, came closer and,
          abruptly, poked me in the ribs.
"I have, I have! Did you think I hadn't? Well, in that
          case you're just wrong,
If that's what you think you're just plain wrong.
          Wrong, I tell you. Wrong!"
He turned and started back into the house. "Are you
          leaving, then?" I wondered, but quietly.
He moved, he spoke, like a man ready to take his
          leave. I could not take it in.
After all these months, after all we had been through
          together?
"Where will you go, Beethoven?" But he was already
          inside, and I was outside still,
And he did not hear me.

Mt. Evans

He did not leave, not then. We drove to the top of
      the tallest mountain I could find,
Next day, drove up and then down again, and on
      the loftiest vehicular road anywhere
In the world: the sign said so, and I believe it.
There was snow in June, and ice, bare rock and lichen;
The road was in fact a glorified mule track; trees had
      long since disappeared.
But we got up there (I never look down, when I drive
      in mountains),
We parked and ate greasy doughnuts and fought the
      flies in the portable toilets
And finally we headed back down. "Well?" I wondered,
As we passed onto the smooth macadam of a
      regular road,
Still above the tree line, still colder than hell, but safe,
      more or less.
We passed a stone lake. We passed a scary rock slide.
We passed fishermen and tourists and other cars,
We passed trucks and trailers and campers and jeeps,
      even a few bicycles, even at fourteen
      thousand feet.
"Well?" I repeated, and Beethoven startled me by
      rolling down his window
And spitting onto the road. The air was acrid, thin.
"That!" he muttered. He sounded angry—not bored:
      angry.
I could not turn and look at him, not on that
      well-surfaced but winding road.
"Is that disappointment, Herr Beethoven?"

He grunted: "That is disgust, Herr Raffel.

Portable privies on such a noble mountain—such a
mountain!

Disgusting. You are no more civilized that we were,
a hundred and fifty years ago."

I chuckled. He was very funny.

"Who ever said we were, eh? Who? Not me, my friend!
Not me!" I sang silently to myself, the rest of the
way home.

I felt fine, I did not worry about Beethoven.

CHOICES

It took a lot of courage to ask Beethoven, finally,
What he thought of modern music. He had heard
      more than enough,
It seemed to me; it was time; his judgment was important;
And I was curious.
"Interesting," was all he would say, until I pushed him.
"Could *you* write like that?" I demanded. "Would you?"
      Will you?"
He was reading the daily paper and did not look up.
      But he smiled.
"I might. Why finish that old *Tenth Symphony,* eh?
      Not now!
Too much has changed. *I've* changed!"
"But you're still Beethoven, you're still a musician,
      damn it."
He nodded, and his smile lingered quietly.
"I'm still Beethoven, anyway," he said almost casually.
"Am I still a musician? I wonder, I do. Who knows, eh?"
I was upset: "Of course you are!" I began, but he
      looked up, at last, and silenced me
With a gentle gesture. "It's really not so easy,
      Herr Raffel,
As I think you ought to know. This world of yours—
Do I *want* to make music for this world?" he chuckled.
"For all my good intentions, you know, I haven't, not
      so far. Will I?
Will I change that much?" he shrugged, visibly
      unconcerned.
"Certainly, I will change more than your world will,
      and a good deal faster.
I think that too is obvious—isn't it obvious, Herr Raffel?"

I tried to stay calm. The greatest musician in the
world, here, now, right in front of me
And virtually forswearing music? "But what *will* you
do, Herr Beethoven?"
He was reading the newspaper again; it took him a
while to answer.
"Do?" He considered. "Well, I might become a
sportswriter—why not?
Or perhaps a computer programmer. I could try
inventing—I have some excellent ideas already.
Or retail fashion—women's fashion, yes: these
advertisements, how fascinating they are!"
He pointed at the paper. His smile was the perfect,
strong Beethoven smile,
Confident, exactly how he had always seemed in
the old drawings, the faded old prints.
"There's so much I could do, Herr Raffel! The
opportunities are vast, are glorious:
I want to be careful with them. How often are we
given this sort of second chance, eh?
Why limit myself? And was music so kind to me,
that first time,
That I need to worry myself on its account? No,
Herr Raffel,
I'll be very careful indeed, this time, more careful, I
assure you, that I ever knew how to be,
Once upon a time." He shook his head mildly.
"Such opportunities, such magnificent opportunities!
How can I pass up any of them? That's the question I
keep asking myself."
He hesitated, then smiled genially. "And I haven't
found the answer, not yet.
Who knows if I ever will, eh? Who knows?"
His face clear, his voice calm, his hands steady,
He went back to his newspaper. I asked him no
more questions.

"You call yourself a poet!" Beethoven raged at me, the
      night I denied angels, and gods, even progress,
And certainly most of what was called beauty.
"In my time, Herr Raffel," he announced with ringing
      clarity, his voice full, his face flushed and his
      lips quivering,
"A poet *believed*, it was belief, and precisely belief,
      which made him more than an ordinary man—
Which made him, my young American friend, a poet."
"Oh," was all I said. "And what do *you* believe?"
      he pursued, leaning toward me,
His chin jutting out.
"A lot of things," I said casually—and it was not a
      pretense, I meant it.
"I guess a lot of them would strike you as pretty
      negative. I can't help that,
Herr Beethoven. But anyway, you're wrong, you know.
Belief can sustain a poet, I suppose, but it sure
      can't make one."
He glowered, nodding with solemn certainty. I wished
      I had his certainty,
I wished anyone alive today still had it. "Ja!" he
      exclaimed, "and what *does* make a poet?"
He refused another beer, his gesture was singularly
      brusque. Maybe he thought I was trying to
      distract him,
Though I was only trying to be polite. I also happen
      to think that beer
Is more important that any abstraction.
We were silent for a moment.

"Two things," I finally said, as dryly as I could. "A
     good ear and a knack for turning phrases."
He stared at me. "That's all?"
"That's all." He put his hands on his square knees and
     slowly shook his head,
I guess more sorrowful, now, than angry. "Ach," he
     sighed, "wei dumm is das!
It is—pathetic. Yes, pathetic." He was proud of using
     the word, his face flowed.
"And how little you have, if that is indeed the case,"
     he added,
"If poetry, glorious poetry, has sunk so low that all it
     can bring you—any of you,
For you, Herr Raffel, are plainly a creature of your
     time, and no more to blame than anyone else
     in your nation—
If all it can bring you is such—*materialism!*"
I considered. "That could be," I admitted.
"But I'm pretty satisfied, I want you to know. I'm used
     to not having very much—
Along those lines, I mean. I guess it suits me."
He sighed a long and heavy sigh, and I wanted to
     smile and did not.
"I should play you something bright and cheerful, I
     should force you to let the spirit flow in your
     veins again—
But there is no piano in this verdamte house, how
     can I do *anything?*"
"Bestimmt," I murmured dryly. "Quite so."
And then he burst into laughter,
And though nothing had changed,
Or would change,
Or could change,
Everything was all right again, at least between us.

Aphorisms and Fragments

Transcribed at random from miscellaneous
conversations with Beethoven

A man can only live in one world at a time.

Music is not the food of the gods—or their speech.
It is a disciplined riot.

What a carpenter calls pain
I call experience.

Children are neither a necessary evil
Nor necessary.

How many men can say "I love you"
To themselves
And mean it?

To ignore the sun—the sky—snow, rain—
Is to ignore oneself: we are the world,
We are all the world there is.

What would Mozart have done, had he lived?
What would poor Schubert have done, had he lived?
These are the wrong questions. Besserzufragen, instead:
What would I have done, had I lived?

If the gods did not drink wine, as scholars say,
They were stupider even than men.

Feet are too much slighted—in your world, especially.
Feet are God's most glorious creation:
To play the piano with one's feet (as one does play
            the organ)
Would be to recreate Heaven on earth.
In the meantime, of course, there is always walking.

I have never liked swans.

Gold should not be left in the ground
Or in one's teeth.
It requires spending to be properly appreciated.

Give me apples, and honey, and good strong cheese:
I'll pay you with a song!

Who cares what makes the world go around?

Happiness is not everything, but all things.

FAREWELL

I should have taken him to see the cherry trees, and
        spring in girls' faces,
And the Grand Canyon and the Lincoln Monument,
And a good baseball game. He could have used all that,
He might have stayed, if I'd been able to show him
        our kind of beauty,
Our sort of spirit in action, maybe even a little nobility,
        somewhere or other.
It's not my style.
I showed him me and my family, my dogs, my
        students, my world, and
Of course it wasn't enough for a man like Beethoven,
And one autumn morning he showed up missing. He
        never sent so much as a postcard
From wherever it was he went to: I never knew,
I never heard from him again. And I've missed him:
Take him all in all, he was the best house guest I
        ever had.
But how could I keep him under false pretenses?
How could I be—no, not even for him!—anything but
        what I was?
And I think Beethoven too wanted it that way,
I think maybe that was why he stayed as long as he did.
But anyway, he's gone, and if anything is or has ever
        been normal around here
It's normal again. For better or worse.
But I do miss him, I miss him very much. We became
        friends, I think,
And whatever he thinks of me, I think he's a lovely man.
He's just lovely for someone else, now, and not for me.

And I suppose I can manage enough generosity to
      share him,
Now that he's crossed a hundred and fifty years and
      come back to us.
I've had my turn: now it's yours.

OTHER POEMS

To the Muses

What to pledge, this damp, this warm and winter
Night? There's snow, in most America,
But here: bananas, fronded palms in inner
Courtyards, roses red in rain. Here errant
Crickets sing in thick dark grass.
                                    I offer
Poet-food for altars, simple bits
Of word, a daisy-chain or two: all for
You and some for me.
                        Unwelcome gifts
For hard-heart Muses! Indifferent gods, you chose
Me, didn't you? Palm leaves raised like bent umbrellas
Shield my head from storms, but no light shows
A road. I fumble, casting useless spells.
No glow will shine. So burn, my poems, my rhymes,
Become my torches, since I'm never sent a sign.

MERCATOR MAGIC

This ragged blob spot, red against the blue
Of background, frames a shape not meant by nature,
Two hundred thousand women, men, and brand-new
Children, flat in cartographic stature.
I sit here, work, go shopping, walking, run.
Ignoring draftsman-conjured scenes, I chew
My three-dimensioned meals, I play with won-
Dering kids, I love my wife, admire the view.

So welcome, truly vital facts, my map-land
Acted out in living color, full
With brilliant sound, displayed with no commercials!
A place not shown in printed pages, wrapped
And handy, sold for profit, dreams, diversions,
Just peaceful, dull, no glamour, glitter, bull.

REPORT FROM EVERYWHERE

And here's where universes end. Wherever
I am, worlds desist an inch in front
Of vision. Sliding slippery circles, never
Sure of footing, working hard at hunting
Planets, moons, and stars unseen before,
But always pacing out the same old story:
No one helps, I've had no guide, the more
I walk the less I know.

               Is there a history?
Something other than this time around
Me?

    Up and down I go, bits of rock
Come falling, nothing stays where first it's found.
This grass will grow forever, never stop.
This air's gone ripe with unfamiliar smells.
Has someone learned the secret?

                  Who can tell?

MAN TALK, ANIMAL LISTEN

Solid jawbones work on wolves, hyenas.
Whales swim seas behind an ivory screen,
Filtering fish all day. A shark machine
Displays long rows of ready teeth, patina-
Free. Gorillas bite off twigs, careen
From tree to tree, and rhinos stuff down leaves
And stems and vines. No lion starts to dream
Without a carcass rotting near him: breeze
And bone-marks point the path. But fragile mouths
Are human signs—for oozing charm, for spraying
Words with lips uniquely Darwin-fine.
Thus homo sapiens builds its niches, out-
Debating worlds. No need to roar our saying:
Guns and tongues can speak persuasive lines.

If Music Be the Food of Love

Are sea-fowls singing sorrow? Whitman thought
So, hearing, out on New York islands, birds
Now separate forever.
                              Forget what ought
To happen: birds don't think of death. What terms
Of clear emotion color songs, non-human
Music sung in sadness, making joy?

They whistle out of skies, from trees, in tune
With wind. Indeed. But tone and pitch are noise,
Not knowledge.
                          What does singing make for? Souls
In pain, in heat, can roar their season, rage
Or yelp, yet nothing fills a hollowed hole,
No song, no words. Rattled bars on cages
Free no locks, release no doors. Passion,
Triumph—fun to pour. But love is always rationed.

AGE

No palsy, no, no neurons dripping out
Your nose, since this is season, not mere state.
Who's found the cure for summer? Who still doubts
How winter follows fall? But different rates
Apply: these icy winds, these ever-burning
Skies will measure passing man, not years.
No winter leads us back, restores us spring.
No birds come soaring out of south, appear
Like life itself, as earth grows fresh, turns green.
Though snow goes soft and melts, here it's ice
Forever. Blossoms, buds are memories, seen
A last time, now no more. Rats and mice
Are good a year or two, men for longer.
Life's a fragile growth, and death is stronger.

WHATEVER'S HARD AND WHITE

Our bones outlast us. Given right conditions,
Heat and cold, now damp, now dry, they last
A million years—stone dead, mere wreckage passed
Along like rocks and fallen trees, position
Nodes for archeologist debate,
Who never argue flesh implies endurance,
Skulls and femurs, teeth, the well-known freight
Of accidental time and change. No sewers
Clog with brains. Intelligence decays
In dew, dissolves in rain, and who we were
We will not be again, just bleached and faded
Calcic ruins, bare.
                           No need to hurry:
Lines we hang on, dessicated rags,
Freeze through time, old, stiff, and glaciated flags.

WINTER

Walkers slow on winter beaches find
Predictable surprises—starfish broken
Open (handy viewing), horseshoe hides
Squashed to cardboard flats. You can't go poking
Sandy jetsam, stunned by blood-stained tokens.
Hook-beaked hungry gulls keep chopping, prying
Fishy gut; you see pale reams of spiders
Crawl in feathered corpses. The word's been spoken
Down the world's thin edge.
                              This season is time
For years both dead and dying to earn their local
Fame, deserve their rotting laurels. Invoking
Prize of bone-bleached branches wreathed in slime,
Inhuman mothers of us all indulge their primal
Skills. They sculpt us birth and death, they teach survival.

Mausoleum Mirrors

Babies look like nothing human, take
On doll-glow fat and softness. Hair and teeth
Accumulate, big eyes acquire fake
Attractive glaze of sense. Then words complete
Illusions. Boys begin as smoothed-out, wrinkle-
Freed, pink-cheeked new reproductions, dad
Reborn, girls as sylph-thin moms. They mingle
Bits of family portraits, fresh, unpadded,
Crisp ancestral faces. Near the end
The visage sprouts from long-dead graves, unlikely
Sights, he his mother's mother spiked
By beard, she some long-dead uncle.
                                    We send
Imperfect messages unmeant, genes
Extruding history, life expressing lives unseen.

CARNIVORES AND PREY

And then the screaming, once the leopards, lions,
Stretch out, stuffed, with fifty pounds of meat
Distending every fur-lined belly? Flying
Panic, febrile fear?
                          No. Just sweetly
Peaceful quiet, birds bright chirp and snapping
Crickets while the sun sets. Flocks reduced
A head or two, but when assassins nap
There's open grazing, room at rivers—proof
Supreme: quick life's the only thing that lasts.

Until it doesn't.

                          Death's a passing glitch,
A flickering fact, mere static. Once it's past
It's gone. Only life goes on, in ditches,
Dirty ponds, green fields or huts, unknown
Immortal fungus, wind forever blowing.

THE FATHERS

Flesh of flesh: oh once upon a name,
When shrunken adults played as models, carved
To tiny scale but cut and shaped the same—
And even Mendel, tending mountains, marbled
Pea-pod flowers, year by year, erased,
Inserted stripes and dots, made generations
Mix and cross, invented bright gestations
As they pleased him, he the new creator,
Fertile, priestly father, monkish man—
Once upon that dead belief, we fancied
Children us, come young again, and planned
To keep us living after lives gone rancid.

      Children are themselves. We fire the gun,
      They start. And then like us they learn to
           run alone.

FOREBEARS

A half millenium ago, and more,
Those unknown men and women brought inchoate
Seeds away, scheming how to pour
Their blood across new time and into flow
And ebb of never-ending now, while keeping
Air in lung-breaths, food in bellies, glow
Of good no longer Spanish soil at feet
And God's great grace in mind, His world in tow,
For Spain had spit them over seas, around
The earth. They flew, while cursing no one, mourning
Olive skies and scent of oranges blooming.
Their children never heard those summer-sounding
Soft-leafed trees, walked in bright-breathed rooms
Where Sancho Panza chattered to his master, nobly born.

Everett Morton Raffel

Could I ignore a brother tall as zooming
Stars, vast as planets, dark eyes scowling
Down from skies and lashing storms, booming,
Blasting lightning, thunder? Everett had powers,
Whipping worlds with pocket chains, flogging
Moons. He drew down rain with crooking fingers,
Melted snow at a glance. His voice clogged
My blood. His angry footsteps stunned like stinging
Blows. I worshipped hard, prayed at shrines
I built in secret, books of praise fat
On ready lips, but all his sacred signs
Fled from juvenile weakness, squeaking bats
Flown from caves of darkness. I lingered blind as broken
Idols, sight extinguished. Love was never spoken.

NATHAN'S TOY ANIMALS

My first sons reared and ruled a royal court,
The king a soft-toy puppy, floppy eared.
My daughters' dolls amused themselves with short-
Legged dogs and rabbits, cats, not ever fearing
Claws on five-foot tigers, eyed in glass
And glaring, buffaloes just two feet high
With small moustaches, lion's teeth (behind
Their velvet mask) high white, and long, and flashing.

But you, Nathan, last-born ever, roll
In Grizzly's arms, pulling silver-tinted
Fur, and chat with dinosaurs, controlling
Duckling lives. You sleep on lamb's soft skin.
Plush and plaster, glass and felt and wood,
Alive and all, godly, great, and good.

Letter to My Dead Son, Blake

Who knows what your life might have been, these twenty
Years? Cancer killed you.
                                  Now it's time,
It's more than time, to tell you, in that empty
Absence you don't live in, what I in prime
Of living on still think of, night and day,
Reconstituting shadows which were you.

Hospital bed, your long thin bones.
                                        Your face
At twelve, running uphill to where I stood.
Listening as you sang your songs.
                                        Laughter,
Playing catch with pillows, brother, me.
Old tears, poured out for childhood's vast disasters.
That stubborn smile, defiantly not guilty.

Your hair, long down your back, knotted, clumped,
         and matted.
Days they let you out,
                          before your body vanished.

HOMESPUN

Whatever day, however weather, let
The skies be colored self, the sun appear
But as it pleases. Ignore hard rain, forget
Fresh frost and frozen snow. Accept the clear
Plain sense of time, of place, which are as are.
Refrain, give up pretending, stop belief.
Only go where nose will lead you: start
To follow breath, and buds of dried-up grief
Will open up like roses.
                  Nothing's real
Until it's known. That belly-buttons grew
You've grasped, but knowledge born of minds just peels
Away as worlds push sharp. You never knew
You walked for walking, talked for talking, lived
For life, as you were born for birth. No more is given.

REVELATION

Not in ditches, not in darkness, rumbling
Wonder blown from night, flaming bright
As flaring stars, brief as God's own humbler
Word (how long since heard!) that brought His light
To barren bowls of early dawn.
Yet there
Were blossoms overhead, a booming thrown
Like lightning in our eyes: what fire appeared?
What revelation burst and then was gone?
Mere millisecond flash of sky, a frozen
Warning, vanished, unreturned.
And who
Are we to seek a vision, blasted bolt
Of reassurance, lost before we knew it?
Now, what reservoirs of knowing feed
Our hearts, except the certainty of need?

And You, My Love

And you, my love, keep passing in and out
Of dreams, wearing smiles and sometimes wearing
More. You come to me from darkness, mouth
Half open, eyes like green-lit torches flaring
Sunlight, nothing trailed behind you, sound-
Less air, the sky against you blue, unsinging
Birds in bare-branched trees. Long hair unwound
Around you. Far-heard silver bells keep ringing.
I see the constellations fall and dip.
Great lights implode, and stars drop burning down.
I hunt you, all alone, I slide and slip,
I find you, lose you. Time goes swinging round,
Around, until, somewhere beneath a moon,
We float together, not too late—

but not too soon.